EXTREME
WHEELS

This book is officially licensed by Winning Moves UK Ltd, owners of the Top Trumps registered trademark.

Tim Oldham has asserted his right to be identified as the author of this book.

British Library Cataloguing-in-Publication Data:
A catalogue record for this book is available from the British Library

ISBN 978 184425 460 6

Library of Congress catalog card no. 2007931171

Published by Haynes Publishing,
Sparkford, Yeovil, Somerset BA22 7JJ, UK
Tel: +44 (0)1963 442030 Fax: +44 (0)1963 440001
Email: sales@haynes.co.uk; Website: www.haynes.co.uk

Haynes North America, Inc.,
861 Lawrence Drive, Newbury Park, California 91320, USA

Printed and bound in Great Britain by J. H. Haynes & Co. Ltd, Sparkford

All photographs courtesy vehicle manufacturers except:

Roland Brown: McLean Monowheel
Giles Chapman: Ford Indigo, Lexus Minority Report, Mercedes Benz
F300 Life-Jet, Renault Espace F1, Renault Zoom
Richard Dredge: Venturi Eclectic
Lisa Morris/Monsterphotos.co.uk: Bigfoot® 17
MTM: Audi TT Bimoto
Spark Engineering BV 2006: PAL-V

The Author

A former features editor of *Top Gear Magazine*, Tim Oldham is a writer and editor spcialising in motoring and sport.

TOP TRUMPS®

EXTREME WHEELS

Contents

About
Top Trumps

It's now more than 30 years since Britain's kids first caught the Top Trumps craze. The game remained hugely popular until the 1990s, when it slowly drifted into obscurity. Then, in 1999, UK games company Winning Moves discovered it, bought it, dusted it down, gave it a thorough makeover and introduced it to a whole new generation. And so the Top Trumps legend continues.

Nowadays, there are Top Trumps titles for just about everyone, with subjects about animals, cars, ships, aircraft and all the great films and TV shows. Top Trumps is now even more popular than before. In Britain, a pack of Top Trumps is bought every six seconds! And it's not just British children who love the game. Children in Australasia, the Far East, the Middle East, all over Europe and in North America can buy Top Trumps at their local shops.

Today you can even play the game on the internet, interactive DVD, your games console and even your mobile phone.

You've played the game...

Now read the book!

Haynes Publishing and Top Trumps have teamed up to bring you this exciting new Top Trumps book, in which you will find even more pictures, details and statistics.

Top Trumps: Extreme Wheels features 45 of the world's fastest, most innovative, futuristic or wacky vehicles, from ultimate production models, made-to-order specials and manufacturers' concepts to weird customs, outrageous conversions and massive monster machines. Packed with fascinating facts, stunning photographs and all the vital statistics, this is the essential pocket guide to the world of extreme motoring.

Look out for other Top Trumps books from Haynes Publishing – even more facts, even more fun!

Acabion
GTBO-70

Acabion
GTBO-70

Imagine you're behind the wheel of a Bugatti Veyron pushing on to that magical 250mph top speed. You're the fastest of the fast. Untouchable. That's until a streamlined jet-fighter canopy on two wheels momentarily appears in your rear-view mirror before zipping past and disappearing into the distance. You've just been smoked by an Acabion GTBO-70. This remarkable vehicle made its debut at the 2006 Geneva Motor Show and goes to show what a light weight carbon fibre frame – just 360kg – and a smooth, low-resistance shape can really do. Oh, once you've factored in that power comes from a turbocharged 1.3-litre engine, dragster-tuned to a demented 700bhp. In this company, 0–60mph is not the ballpark. With around 2000bhp per ton, the GTBO–70 is estimated to blitz from rest to 280mph in 19 seconds. And did we mention that there's plenty of boot space for luggage and a staggering return of 85mpg with low carbon dioxide emissions? Before you ask, those rear stabilisers are just that – balance for walking speed manoeuvres. And if you think this is insane, take a look at the RS-F – it's what Acabion has got planned for the next generation of SUV.

Statistics

Type of vehicle:	two-seater missile
Year:	2006
Country of origin:	Switzerland
Length:	4640mm
Width:	900mm
Height:	1200mm
Weight:	360kg
Engine type:	1.3-litre turbo
Max power:	700bhp
Max speed:	375mph (limited to 293mph)
Number of seats:	2
Special features:	insane speed and 85mpg
Extreme rating:	9

Audi TT
Bimoto

Audi TT
Bimoto

Germany isn't short of specialist tuners who are more than happy to extract a bit of extra performance from your standard road car. Brabus and AMG are easily the best known of these outfits, so when Roland Meyer – head honcho at MTM – wanted to create a stir, he knew he had to come up with something special. And with the MTM Bimoto he certainly did that. There was nothing particularly special about his base car – an Audi TT – but the fact that he chose to fit it with two engines, making the MTM Bimoto one of the most extreme road cars on the planet. Each engine retains its own gearbox – the front engine powers the front wheels and the one behind looks after the rear ones (the rear seats have been removed to make room). However, the gearboxes are operated in sync so there won't be any comedy moments of the front of the car pulling away from the rear. There's the slightly quirky sight of two starter buttons on the dashboard, but they probably serve to remind the driver – should they forget – that with each 1.8l four-cylinder turbo engine producing 370bhp, they have the combined thrust of around 740bhp to unleash. It's only when you've get this sort of power to play with that the rarely used 0–300km/h comes into play. It's a shade under 20sec if you're asking. The TT has already topped 230mph at the Nardo test track, putting it into some truly exalted company – such as Brabus and AMG for example.

Statistics

Type of vehicle:	two-seater coupé
Year:	2002
Country of origin:	Germany
Length:	4041mm
Width:	1764mm
Height:	1348mm
Weight:	1490kg
Engine type:	2 x 1.8-litre turbos
Max power:	740bhp
Max speed:	230mph
Number of seats:	2
Special features:	it's got two of everything important
Extreme rating:	9

No list of extreme vehicles could be complete without Bigfoot® – the original monster truck. Ever since St Louis construction contractor Bob Chandler started his own 4x4 parts business in the early 1970s and built Bigfoot® 1 as a promotional vehicle, it's stamped its huge tyre-print on popular culture. Back in 1981, Chandler drove Bigfoot® 1 over the top of a couple of junk cars. It fuelled an explosion of interest and a new, err 'sport' was born. Many imitators have tried to take it on, but Bigfoot® has crushed them all. Since Bigfoot® 1, there has been a whole spate of Bigfoots® (except a number 13 which is considered unlucky). For sheer size, Bigfoot® 5 takes all the beating, while Bigfoot® 14 is the undisputed king of the jumps – clearing 202 feet. And as it became clear that due to a very heavy appearance schedule in the USA, no existing Bigfoot® could be available for a European tour, Bob Chandler collaborated on a Bigfoot® for use in Europe called Bigfoot® 17 – the UK's own Bigfoot®. Completed in 2003, Bigfoot® 17 has been entertaining fans across Europe in the European Monster Truck Racing Championship.

Statistics

Type of vehicle:	monster truck
Year:	2003
Country of origin:	UK
Length:	5486mm
Width:	3810mm
Height:	3048mm
Weight:	4309kg
Engine type:	572 cubic inch Ford V8 supercharged
Max power:	1750bhp
Max speed:	80mph
Number of seats:	1
Special features:	renowed car crusher
Extreme rating:	8

BMW
H2R

BMW
H2R

As a fuel, hydrogen answers many environmental issues. The clean burning process of liquid hydrogen combustion produces no harmful emissions, there's no danger to the atmosphere, and hydrogen can be produced from a variety of renewable resources. And with its streamliner racer, the H2R, BMW has shown just what the hydrogen car is able to offer in terms of performance. Whereas some people have gone down the route of hydrogen fuel cells, BMW has gone for a traditional engine – its 6.0-litre 12-cylinder engine taken from the BMW 760i – and adapted it for a non-quite-so-traditional fuel. It operates on the same principle as other internal combustion engines, but the main modifications involve the fuel injection system being adapted to the special requirements of hydrogen. Stretching 5.4m in length, the body of the H2R is designed for optimal streamlining and stability at high speed. It also looks amazing in its outer skin made from carbon-fibre reinforced plastic for stiffness and low weight. In September 2004, the H2R set nine world records for hydrogen-powered cars. The engine technology in the H2R Record Car enables delivery of 232bhp and a 0–62mph time of six seconds with a top speed of 187.62mph.

Statistics

Type of vehicle:	hydrogen powered prototype
Year:	2004
Country of origin:	Germany
Length:	5400mm
Width:	2000mm
Height:	-
Weight:	1560kg (with driver)
Engine type:	6-litre V12 modified for hydrogen combustion
Max power:	232bhp
Max speed:	187.622mph
Number of seats:	1
Special features:	a clean, green performer
Extreme rating:	6

Brabus
Rocket

Brabus
Rocket

No doubt you'll already have heard of German tuning company Brabus. They take perfectly decent and normal Mercedes and turn them into fire-breathing monsters. And this CLS-based example is no exception. Thanks to a 6.3-litre V12 twin-turbo shoehorned under that bonnet, this is officially the fastest four-door street-legal saloon on the planet. Unsurprisingly, it's called the Brabus Rocket. During test runs at the high-speed track in Nardo, Italy, the 730bhp Rocket was clocked at 227mph (362.4km/h). That's faster than a Pagani Zonda, Lamborghini Murciélago and Ferrari Enzo. What's so extreme about this sort of speed is that more than two of you can share the experience. Nor is the Rocket any slouch in reaching that terminal velocity. It accelerates from 0–62mph (100km/h) in four seconds, 125mph (200km/h) comes up in a staggering 10.5 seconds, and 186mph (300km/h) in just under 30 seconds. It's close to time travel performance. Bespoke light-alloy wheels, powerful carbon ceramic brakes, modified suspension and newly programmed engine electronics, are all part of the Brabus engineers' treatment, while the design department custom developed a front apron for the Rocket with large air inlets to help with cooling and aerodynamic stability.

Statistics

Type of vehicle:	**four-door saloon**
Year:	**2005**
Country of origin:	**Germany**
Length:	**4915mm**
Width:	**1873mm**
Height:	**1389mm**
Weight:	**1980kg**
Engine type:	**6.3-litre V12 twin-turbo**
Max power:	**730bhp**
Max speed:	**227mph**
Number of seats:	**4**
Special features:	**there's a police car version!**
Extreme rating:	**7**

Bugatti
Veyron

Bugatti
Veyron

You know things are a little out of the ordinary when Ferraris, Astons or Rolls-Royces are made to look like something out of the bargain basement. Yes, when it comes to extremes of expense, we're into the rarified atmosphere of the super-rich. Here you'll find Pagani Zondas, Maybachs and the Koenigsegg. But comfortably topping the list of the world's most expensive production cars is the Bugatti Veyron 16.4, yours for a cool 1M euros. The Veyron also looks down on everyone else when it comes to categories for most powerful and fastest production car too. The W16 engine – 16 cylinders in four banks of four – produces around 990bhp (twice that of your average supercar) and propels the exquisitely built machine to a top speed of 253mph. That's faster top end than a Formula 1 car. The seven-gear all-wheel-drive Veyron is so fast that engineers customised three different suspension modes. From the standard setting – that's below 136mph – the driver can engage a second mode where the body drops closer to the ground and the tail wing is deployed. For speeds above 233mph, you have to manually activate the lowered setting with a key. Yet despite its cost, Bugatti admit they won't make any money from the Veyron. It's all part of a big plan to bring back the Bugatti brand.

Statistics

Type of vehicle:	**two-door coupé**
Year:	**2006**
Country of origin:	**Germany**
Length:	**4462mm**
Width:	**1998mm**
Height:	**1204mm**
Weight:	**1888kg**
Engine type:	**8-litre W16 with four turbochargers**
Max power:	**987bhp**
Max speed:	**253mph**
Number of seats:	**2**
Special features:	**looks sensational**
Extreme rating:	**7**

Caparo
T1

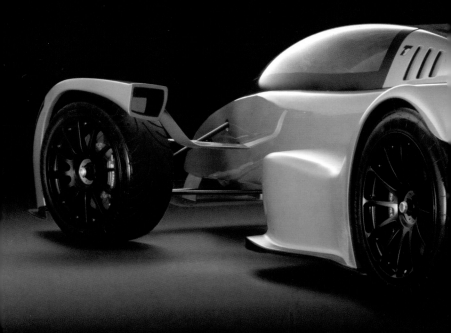

Caparo T1

Other than stick indicators and headlights onto Lewis Hamilton's Mclaren MP4-22, the Caparo T1 is the nearest thing you'll get to an F1 car on the road. The T1 is the brainchild of Ben Scott Geddes and Graham Halstead, both of whom worked on the McLaren F1 road car project. Now, the pair have created an awesomely styled and ultra-lightweight road car that will provide stunning levels of performance. Engineering genius behind the McLaren F1, Gordon Murray, has also recently joined the T1 team. That's pedigree. Using carbon fibre for the monocoque and other lightweight materials throughout, the T1 strips down to an impressively lean 550kg. Powered by a bespoke 3.5-litre normally-aspirated fuel-injected V8 that produces 575bhp and you've got a car that boasts a power-to-weight ratio of over 1000bhp per tonne. That said, expect this British-designed and built car to flash past 60mph in 2.5sec, 100mph in 5sec and top out at 200mph. There's huge brakes to match. But what makes the performance so extreme is that the advanced aerodynamic package allows cornering forces of up to 3g. Better get down the gym and work on those neck muscles. The price is expected to be around the £190,000 mark.

Statistics

Type of vehicle:	**F1 car for the road**
Year:	**2006**
Country of origin:	**UK**
Length:	**4066mm**
Width:	**1924mm**
Height:	**1076mm**
Weight:	**550kg**
Engine type:	**3.5-litre V8**
Max power:	**575bhp**
Max speed:	**200mph**
Number of seats:	**2**
Special features:	**F1 style g-forces**
Extreme rating:	**8**

Casual
LoFa

Casual LoFa

In truth, any of Edd China's remarkable collection of motorised weirdness is deserved of the word extreme, but the Casual Lofa makes it here because it remains the original and best. Okay, so it's recently lost its tag as the world's fastest furniture, but the leopard print sofa knocks the others dead with its road presence and inventive features. These include a drinks can brake pedal, a chocolate bar gear selector and a knee-operated throttle should you decide to relax and ease back in your driving position. The front indicators are inside plant pots, while the coffee table not only acts as a front bumper but also holds the speedo and a working television. It's still hard to imagine how it ever qualified as street legal. That said, the mid-mounted Mini engine has eased it to thousands of comfortable miles – including a world record for furniture of 87mph in 1998, which stood until May 2007. Other weird and wonderful cars from the China stable at his company Cummfy Banana include a motorised four-poster bed, a toilet bike and bath sidecar combination, and a fur-covered VW Beetle.

Statistics

Type of vehicle:	**motorised sofa**
Year:	**1999**
Country of origin:	**UK**
Length:	**2200mm**
Width:	**1800mm**
Height:	**1200mm (1900mm including lamp)**
Weight:	**800kg**
Engine type:	**1.3-litre fuel injection**
Max power:	**65bhp**
Max speed:	**87mph (a world record!)**
Number of seats:	**3**
Special features:	**telly, standard lamp**
Extreme rating:	**6**

Citroën
C-Metisse

Citroën
C-Metisse

Exploring new paths dedicated to automotive pleasure – that's how Citroën sums up this wacky four-door coupé, with its wide and low bodywork, flamboyant but still elegant, its spectacular door design and its chrome-dripping details. However, under its swoopy contours, the hardware is deadly serious stuff. It features a specially designed high-performance hybrid drivetrain, with a diesel engine harnessed to a pair of electric motors which are installed actually inside the rear wheels for the ultimate in road grip…and, of course, excellent environmental credentials. Inside, the large cabin has a touch of nightclub glamour to it, with all four inviting seats richly padded and upholstered in white leather; chocolate bars are definitely banned here! The Michelin wheels not only look good but even the tyres have been designed to have an optimum aerodynamic profile. Meanwhile, the doors perform an almost ballet-like sequence when they open: the front ones are gullwing types, the rear ones rotate backwards, and even the boot opens with a parallelogram action. Each seat has independent air-conditioning controls – stamped into the leather door panels – along with individual roof lighting. The diesel combustion engine: the V6 HDi DPFS, mated to a 6-speed automatic gearbox drives the front wheels, while the dual electric engines are at the back. A 'boost' function gives rapid acceleration and, as it uses both power systems, temporary four-wheel drive.

Statistics

Type of vehicle:	hybrid four-door coupé
Year:	2006
Country of origin:	France
Length:	4741mm
Width:	2001mm
Height:	1241mm
Weight:	1400kg
Engine type:	3-litre V6, diesel-electric hybrid
Max power:	208bhp
Max speed:	155mph (0–60mph in 6.2sec)
Number of seats:	4
Special features:	gullwing *and* scissor doors, electric motors in the rear wheels
Extreme rating:	7

CLEVER

CLEVER

People have been building three-wheeler cars for over a hundred years but they've often been viewed as a rather eccentric way to travel. They've looked odd, too. These days, however, the benefits of low emissions, compact size and radical styling is attracting fresh interest in the three-wheeler market – particularly so for city driving. The CLEVER (that's compact low emission vehicle for urban transport) is a project involving nine European partners from industry and research including BMW and the University of Bath. Still at the prototype stage, the super slippery body consists of a lightweight aluminium chassis with a plastic shell and is powered by compressed natural gas stored in two cylinders behind the passenger's seat. We're talking about low emissions and convenience here rather than extreme performance. Even wiith a kerb weight of just 395kg and a width of less than one metre, the CLEVER will slip through the air to a top speed of 62mph. with its 1+1 seating arrangement and a computer-controlled hydraulic system in which the cabin tilts into a corner to provide plenty of stability, it's sure to be a hoot to drive.

Statistics

Type of vehicle:	three-wheeler prototype
Year:	2006
Country of origin:	EU
Length:	3066mm
Width:	998mm
Height:	1388mm
Weight:	395kg
Engine type:	single-cylinder 230cc natural gas
Max power:	12.5kW
Max speed:	60mph
Number of seats:	2
Special features:	CO_2 emissions less that 60g/km
Extreme rating:	4

Dodge
RAM SRT-10

Dodge
RAM SRT-10

You might think 'what's a pick-up truck doing with a rear spoiler?' Well, you'll find it's got everything to do with the 8.3-litre V10 engine sitting up front. The Dodge RAM SRT-10 was devised as the most powerful and fastest production pick-up ever and the 8.3-litre V10 engine endorses that claim with a class-demolishing 500 horsepower and 525lb ft of torque – topping 150mph and reaching 60mph in just over 5 seconds. So that's the acceleration of a supercar, with the seating capacity of a 4x4, and the load-shifting ability of a Toyota Tacoma. In February 2004, an unmodified RAM SRT-10 took its place in the Guinness World Records with an average speed of 154.587mph. Since then HSV's LS2 6.0-litre V8 Maloo R8 Ute has upped the mark to nearly 170mph, but in our book the RAM is still the baddest truck on the block.

Statistics

Type of vehicle:	double-cab pick-up
Year:	2004
Country of origin:	USA
Length:	5158mm
Width:	2030mm
Height:	1890mm
Weight:	2267kg
Engine type:	8.3-litre V10
Max power:	500bhp
Max speed:	150mph
Number of seats:	5
Special features:	smokin' performance
Extreme rating:	7

MK56 HNJ

Dodge
Tomahawk

Dodge
Tomahawk

Visitors to the North American International Auto Show are used to scene-stealing concepts. They expect to see something exciting and different. Well, in 2003, they got all that and more with the arrival on stage of the mind-blowing Dodge Tomahawk. First, it looked incredible – a four-wheel, single passenger motorbike seemingly honed out of polished aluminium – a brutal piece of rolling sculpture. But what made the Tomahawk such an extreme proposition was that the normally conservative car executives had taken their biggest engine – an 8.3-litre V10 – and effectively built a motorbike around it. It was as close as any vehicle can come to being nothing but riding a big engine. It was engineering genius let rip. The 500bhp V10 Viper engine sits on a billet aluminium body – each part a one-off custom design – and is theoretically capable of speeds in excess of 300mph. Fancy giving that a try? The Dodge philosophy has always been to 'grab life by the horns'. In the case of the Tomahawk, you'd be wise to grab onto anything and everything you can. A reproduction Tomahawk was available to buy in the prestigious Neiman Marcus Christmas Book for around $500,000. You couldn't ride it, however.

Statistics

Type of vehicle:	motorbike
Year:	2003
Country of origin:	USA
Length:	2591mm
Width:	704mm
Height:	937mm
Weight:	680kg
Engine type:	Viper 8.3-litre V10
Max power:	500bhp
Max speed:	300mph plus
Number of seats:	1
Special features:	simply the maddest motorbike ever
Extreme rating:	8

EDAG
GenX

EDAG
GenX

I'm not so sure there are really that many people in the world crying out for a supercar that provides a full-size bed for the driver. But who cares? The fact that someone came up with the idea in the first place, and then built one is good enough. The EDAG GenX was first shown at the 2004 Geneva Motor Show and is one of a series of innovative vehicle concepts from German engineering company and prototype builder EDAG. The show car was conceived as an answer to the social needs of future generations, reflecting the changes in living, working and leisure time. The GenX has been designed with all-wheel-drive and features adjustable ride height to enable it to go off-road too. But the real showpiece is the bed which runs the length of the car. To transform from sleek supercar to camper van, the electrically operated roof is raised to enlarge the interior space and create room to stretch out in comfort. What's more, those shiny external cases fitted to the tapered waist can be removed and used as suitcases, office packs or camping packs.

Statistics

Type of vehicle:	**two-seater sports car with bed**
Year:	**2004**
Country of origin:	**Germany**
Length:	**4466mm**
Width:	**1920mm**
Height:	**1230mm**
Weight:	**-**
Engine type:	**-**
Max power:	**-**
Max speed:	**-**
Number of seats:	**2**
Special features:	**full length bed**
Extreme rating:	**7**

Fiat
Oltre

Fiat
Oltre

You usually associate the Fiat name with stylish and efficient city cars. Certainly nothing as vulgar as an off-roader. That all changed with Fiat's no frills concept 4x4, the Oltre. With its aggressive, purposeful design, the Oltre looks more than capable of taking on the Hummer. And like the Hummer, it shares an impressive military pedigree. The Oltre is derived from the Iveco Light Multirole Vehicle (LMV), the new military off-roader that has been chosen for service use in both the British Army and the Italian Army. It's fair to say that those vehicles will dispense with the luxury fittings of the concept car, but it has clearly inherited all the features peculiar to the military model, starting with the permanent 4x4 transmission that allows it to tackle any route, and the massive 50cm ground clearance. The three-litre diesel engine delivers maximum power of 185bhp which will shift the seven-tonne car to a top speed of 80mph. But for extreme off-roaders like this, that's not the issue. It's as an authentic explorer where the Fiat Oltre shines.

Statistics

Type of vehicle:	off-roader
Year:	2005
Country of origin:	Italy
Length:	4870mm
Width:	2200mm
Height:	2050mm
Weight:	7 tonnes
Engine size:	3.0-litre diesel
Engine type:	4-cylinder in-line
Max power:	185bhp
Max speed:	80mph
Number of seats:	5
Special features:	50cm ground clearance
Extreme rating:	6

Ford
Airstream

Ford
Airstream

If you've always wanted to drive a car that looks like a 1960s sci-fi spaceship then you'd better start praying Ford take their Airstream beyond the concept stage. And, sorry to say, that's unlikely, although everything about this crossover vehicle is based on viable technology. As the name suggests, the Airstream takes its bold, polished design from the classic American trailers that became icons of the American road. And it's the future of the 'road trip' where this vehicle lies – aiming to seduce young families and the soon-to-be-retired with its sense of optimism and adventure. Although the asymmetric side hatch and clam shell doors are one-offs, the plug-in hybrid hydrogen fuel cell powerplant is more than a concept. Ford's HySeries Drive operates under electric power at all times, charges overnight and if the juice runs out while being driven, the hydrogen-powered fuel cell takes over. The interior is no less futuristic and, like the exterior, takes its influences from the film *2001: A Space Odyssey* with the cocoon-like lounge featuring a cool 360-degree viewing screen and even a modern day lava lamp. Just goes to show that extreme styling isn't limited to supercars.

Statistics

Type of vehicle:	crossover
Year:	2007
Country of origin:	USA
Length:	4700mm
Width:	2004mm
Height:	1778mm
Weight:	-
Engine type:	hybrid hydrogen fuel cell
Max power:	-
Max speed:	-
Number of seats:	5
Special features:	just look at it
Extreme rating:	7

Ford
FAB 1

FAB 1

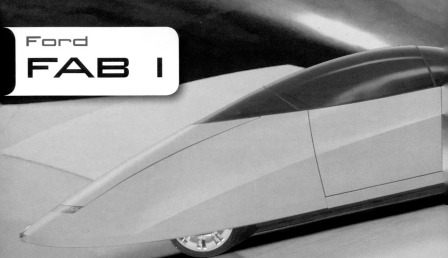

Ford
FAB 1

You can't get much more extreme than a bright pink, 8.2m, two-seater limo. People are going to look. Which is odd really as this is meant to be the carriage of a top secret British agent. But then, this is Thunderbirds. When it came to a film version of the much-loved puppet inhabitants of Tracy Island, the production team first turned to Rolls Royce to create a new FAB 1 – but they were too busy with the Phantom. However, Ford leapt at the chance – they already had the iconic Ford Thunderbird on their fleet. The resulting six-wheel, bubble canopy limo is powered by a not insubstantial 7.4-litre V8 with a natty roof and door-opening action. The interior is fantastic – all chrome and leather – while the 24-inch rims and blacked out glass is pure bling. And it's road legal. Of course, once the film's special efffects team got their hands on it, the car was able to fly and transform into a hydrofoil – all with an impressive arsenal of weapons.

Statistics

Type of vehicle:	**pink six-wheeler for discreet passage of secret agent**
Year:	**2004**
Country of origin:	**USA**
Length:	**8200mm**
Width:	**2000mm**
Height:	**1230mm**
Weight:	**1500kg**
Engine type:	**7.4-litre V8**
Max power:	**classified**
Max speed:	**250mph**
Number of seats:	**2**
Special features:	**bulletproof glass canopy roof, hydrofoils and Vortex-Aquajet Power (for travel on water)**
Extreme rating:	**8**

Ford
Indigo

Ford
Indigo

Not surprisingly, the Ford Indigo V12 concept sports car took its design and technology inspiration from the race track – principally the US Indy Car series. Only two versions of the car were ever produced – a non-driveable show car and a much more interesting fully functioning and driveable model nicknamed the 'Go'. Back in 1996, this radically styled racer was a showcase for new materials and construction techniques, as well as powertrain and aerodynamics. The monocoque chassis was developed by race specialists Reynard Motorsport as a single piece 'tub' made of a carbon fibre composite material – although it was modified slightly to allow for a two-person layout. The scissor doors looked cool, as did the pencil thin indicators and high-intensity headlights. And while the all-new 6-litre V12 engine had an output of 435bhp, it was also expected to return 28mpg under 'normal' driving conditions. Question is, who would want to drive this car under normal conditions? Certainly not the mass of gaming fans who unlocked the Indigo's potential in such console favourites as *Need for Speed II* and *Project Gotham Racing 3*.

Statistics

Type of vehicle:	two-seater race car
Year:	1996
Country of origin:	USA
Length:	4453mm
Width:	2052mm
Height:	1003mm
Weight:	1043kg
Engine type:	5.9-litre V12
Max power:	435bhp
Max speed:	200mph (estimated) (0–60 in 3.8sec)
Number of seats:	2
Special features:	simplicity of design
Extreme rating:	7

Fuel Vapor
Alé

Fuel Vapor
Alé

Okay, so it looks a little like someone's forgotten to build the rest of the car from the cockpit back, but once you've got over its looks the real beauty of the Alé (alay) lies in its ingenious fuel-burning ability. The boffins at Fuel Vapor Technologies in Canada claim that the Alé could make the 800-mile trip from Vancouver to San Francisco on a single 10-gallon tank of fuel. In fact, this prototype has already turned in 92mpg and qualifies for a super-low emissions rating in Canada. All on regular petrol. There's a clue in the name of the company as the Alé runs on fuel vapour rather than normal liquid fuel. It allows the engine to run on a much leaner mixture of fuel and air, yet uses about a third less petrol for the same given power. Best of all, it's great fun to drive. Looking a bit squid-like from above, the Alé's two front wheels drive and steer the car. This gives it great cornering ability, while the additional factors of light weight and smooth aerodynamics enable the Alé to hit 60mph from rest in five seconds and comfortably charge on to a limited 140mph. Fuel Vapor is busy testing the Alé before it goes on sale in 2008.

Statistics

Type of vehicle:	low emission three-wheeler
Year:	2007
Country of origin:	Canada
Length:	4420mm
Width:	2794mm
Height:	1270mm
Weight:	635kg
Engine type:	1.5-litre turbo
Max power:	180bhp
Max speed:	140mph limited
Number of seats:	2
Special features:	innovative new technology
Extreme rating:	6

Holden
EFIJY

Holden
EFIJY

When it comes to finding extremes of speed or size, there's usually very little debate. It's either fast or it isn't. But what about selecting something based on style? Here, one person's idea of radical automotive design may be seen as distinctly ordinary by another. That is, until they lay eyes on the Holden EFIJY. Then, all bets are off. How can anyone not fall in love with this car? The EFIJY was designed and built entirely in-house at Holden's Australian factory. The styling on the car, led by Holden's chief designer Richard Ferlazzo, celebrates Australia's first automotive icon, the 1950s Holden FJ, and incorporates state-of-the-art technology within the beautifully crafted bodywork. Ferlazzo had been scribbling down ideas for his dream car since 1989 and he assembled a design team that clearly shared his vision and enthusiasm. Underneath the amazing pillarless coupé bodywork is a modified Corvette chassis, while a GM 6-litre V8 with supercharger supplies a claimed 645bhp of thrust. And therein lies the real beauty of the EFIJY. It's not just for display. It can really go. Those guys at *Hot Rod Magazine* appreciate craft and detail and made it their Hot Rod of the Year. Praise indeed.

Statistics

Type of vehicle:	21st century hot rod
Year:	2005
Country of origin:	Australia
Length:	5113mm
Width:	1981mm
Height:	1371mm
Weight:	-
Engine type:	6-litre V8 with supercharger
Max power:	645bhp
Max speed:	-
Number of seats:	2
Special features:	it's drop dead gorgeous
Extreme rating:	9

Hummer
H1

Hummer
H1

The Hummer's military might means it rides roughshod over the rules governing most regular production cars, but its overtly combative appearance makes one thing clear: this is warfare on wheels. The High Mobility Multi-Purpose Wheeled Vehicle military vehicle was designed to a 1979 US army blueprint. Its acronym of HMMWV was often referred to as "Humvee", which led to the "Hummer" nickname. Of course, the vehicle was never styled at all, more mapped out so it could resist – literally – anything thrown at it. It didn't have to be that fast, just unstoppable. The 1991 Gulf War was the Hummer's public launch advertising campaign, as the khaki giants were witnessed on worldwide TV liberating Kuwait from Iraqi invasion. In 1992, a 'civilian' model was introduced, eventually known as the H1. It had a detuned Chevrolet Corvette petrol V8, but this was soon replaced by a 6.2-litre GM diesel. It cost up to $45,000 and came in four body configurations, including a four-door soft-top, and with items not found on army models, like seatbelts! The Hummer's automatic tyre deflation and inflation system provided ideal pressures for the prevailing terrain. The Hummer was designed specifically for off-road driving. At 14 inches wider even than the widest Chevrolet sedan, conducting this bulging beast along the high street is only for the most skilled drivers. Nonetheless, Arnold Schwarzenegger was tempted...

Statistics

Type of vehicle:	military-derived off-roader
Year:	1992
Country of origin:	USA
Length:	4686mm
Width:	2197mm
Height:	1905mm
Weight:	3245kg
Engine type:	6.2-litre V8, diesel
Max power:	195bhp
Max speed:	87mph (0–60mph in 17.3sec)
Number of seats:	4
Special features:	approach angle of 73 degrees means the Hummer can go just about anywhere, system for automatically deflating and inflating tyres
Extreme rating:	7

HUMMER

Idea
KAZ

Idea
KAZ

Okay, the KAZ sounds and looks too strange for words, a sort of stretch MPV with low-rider suspension. It seats eight people within its spacious interior and is zero-emission thanks to eight in-wheel electric motors. But although this sounds the perfect vehicle for a sedate cruise around town with a bunch of mates, the KAZ is actually far more at home on a race track. Here, those eight powerful motors produced the electronic equivalent of nearly 600bhp – sufficient to wind the 2980kg KAZ up to an astonishing 193mph. It holds the road well too, thanks to eight-wheel drive. The limo runs on lithium-ion batteries – 84 of them – which are integrated into the car's floorpan and good for a full 180 miles before needing to be recharged. First shown at the 2001 Geneva Motor Show, the KAZ (Keio Advanced Zero-emission vehicle) was developed by researchers in Japan although the car's distinctive styling was the work of IDEA – one of Italy's leading design houses. In some ways, the KAZ was a bit too extreme for people to get their head around and the hoped for orders never materialised.

Statistics

Type of vehicle:	**eight-wheel electric super-stretch**
Year:	**2001**
Country of origin:	**Japan**
Length:	**6700mm**
Width:	**1950mm**
Height:	**1650mm**
Weight:	**2980kg**
Engine type:	**8 electric motors (one per wheel)**
Max power:	**590bhp/440kW (55kW per wheel)**
Max speed:	**193mph**
Number of seats:	**8**
Special features:	**the strange coupling of looks and performance**
Extreme rating:	**9**

International
CXT

International
CXT

If any vehicle makes a pressing claim for inclusion here, it has to be one with 'extreme' in its name. And who's going to say no? Even in a country where oversize pick-ups are the norm, the International CXT (XT is the Extreme bit) is a towering, hugely purposeful workhorse used to getting its own way. Launched in 2004, the CXT is the world's largest production pick-up, capable of hauling six tons – some three times the payload of consumer pick-ups. This industrial strength heritage is derived from a model range of International trucks that are designed for such demanding applications as construction and snowplough. So when you've finished treating Hummers as speed bumps, the CXT's dumping, towing and tilt bed capability might come in very handy. For all its industrial appeal, the CXT is actually rather a luxurious place to be. Once you've scaled the steps into the cabin you'll find leather seats, wood grain trim and a drop-down screen DVD player.

Statistics

Type of vehicle:	**pick-up**
Year:	**2004**
Country of origin:	**USA**
Length:	**6553mm**
Width:	**2590mm**
Height:	**2743mm**
Weight:	**6577kg**
Engine type:	**7.6-litre turbo diesel**
Max power:	**300bhp**
Max speed:	**-**
Number of seats:	**5**
Special features:	**king of the road appeal**
Extreme rating:	**5**

Jay Leno's Ecojet

Jay Leno's
Ecojet

To be honest, it was practically impossible to choose between Jay Leno's 1600bhp tank-engined chrome dragster – appropriately called Tank Car – or his equally unforgettable Ecojet. Neither are elegant but the vote goes to the Ecojet seeing as the TV chat show host had a big hand in bringing it to life. An avid car enthusiast and collector, Leno first discussed the idea of a turbine-powered supercar with his chief mechanic, before convincing GM's Design Studio in LA to take the rough sketches and turn them into a working car. It helps to know people in high places. Designed and produced in collaboration with Leno, his Big Dog team of mechanics, and GM, the EcoJet is powered by a Honeywell LT-101 turbine engine – similar to that found inside Coast Guard helicopters. The Leno original is good for 650bhp and runs on biodiesel. 'At least we're not using fossil fuel. You drive it, then wait around for the next harvest,' says Leno. The engine sits in a modified Corvette Z06 aluminium frame and the vehicle's shell is a construction of carbon fibre and kevlar. As for performance, there's every chance this one-off special could see off a Toyota Prius.

Statistics

Type of vehicle:	**turbine-powered supercar**
Year:	**2006**
Country of origin:	**USA**
Length:	**4674mm**
Width:	**2024mm**
Height:	**1180mm**
Weight:	**-**
Engine type:	**Honeywell LT-101 turbine**
Max power:	**650bhp**
Max speed:	**-**
Number of seats:	**2**
Special features:	**eco-friendly performance**
Extreme rating:	**7**

JCB
Dieselmax

JCB
Dieselmax

You won't see this JCB for dust. Nothing new there, then – after all, we're used to the bright yellow machines tearing up the earth. However, while most JCBs potter along at 20mph, the Dieselmax has managed over 17 times that. What's more, on 23 August 2006, JCB Dieselmax was officially timed as the fastest diesel 'car' ever when it snatched the world record at 350.092mph. Only a few days earlier, it had streaked across the Bonneville Salt Flats in Utah, USA at over 300mph in testing – already way better than the previous fastest diesel, Virgil Snyder's Thermo King Streamliner that achieved 235.756mph in 1973. This time, former RAF pilot and world land speed record holder Andy Green was at the helm. The arrow-like Dieselmax was conceived by company boss Sir Anthony Bamford as an excellent way to prove the British engineering excellence behind it. Believe it or not, this is the Staffordshire company's very own design for a land speed record car. But while the rugged, 4.4-litre, four-cylinder motor gives JCB's usual slow-moving industrial giants a maximum 140bhp, the Dieselmax's version has been reworked to give 750bhp. What's more, the four-wheel drive Dieselmax has two of them, one at the front and one at the back, co-ordinated via a unique transmission system.

Statistics

Type of vehicle:	speed-record car
Year:	2006
Country of origin:	UK
Length:	9091mm
Width:	1145mm
Height:	979mm
Weight:	2700kg
Engine type:	two 4.4-litre four-cylinder, diesel
Max power:	750bhp
Max speed:	350.092mph (0–60mph n/a – it needs to be pushed to 40mph by a tractor – but it can do 100–200mph in 13sec)
Number of seats:	1
Special features:	two diesel engines, two parachute brakes
Extreme rating:	9

Jeep
Hurricane

Jeep Hurricane

The 5.7-litre HEMI engine is capable of delivering 335bhp and 370lb ft of torque. Plenty, you'd imagine, for any vehicle. Well, not for the concept Jeep Hurricane, which blew onto the scene in 2005 with two Hemis – one in the front and one in the back. That's 670bhp and 740lb ft of torque – the sort of torque that enables the Hurricane to climb obstacles that other 4x4s can only dream about. If you're in a hurry, that power and traction will destroy 0–60mph in under five seconds. But it's really as an extreme off-roader that the Hurricane is so highly rated and there are plenty of clever bits in its locker. The Hurricane is equipped with four-wheel independent steering – meaning that each wheel can turn separately from the others. In one mode, the rear wheels turn in the same direction as the front wheels, meaning the Hurricane can 'crab-steer' – move to the side without changing the direction it faces. Another mode allows all four wheels to point-in, allowing the Hurricane to actually rotate in one place. It's a vehicle well-suited to the great outdoors although it's not expected to be a production model – certainly not in quite the extreme form it was introduced.

Statistics

Type of vehicle:	extreme off-roader
Year:	2005
Country of origin:	USA
Length:	3856mm
Width:	2033mm
Height:	1732mm
Weight:	1746kg (estimated)
Engine type:	two 5.7-litre Hemi engines
Max power:	670bhp
Max speed:	120mph (0–60 in under 5sec)
Number of seats:	2
Special features:	can climb anything
Extreme rating:	7

KTM
X-Bow

KTM
X-Bow

KTM is an Austrian motorbike manufacturer with an unrivalled heritage in producing off-road bikes – machines that have enjoyed outstanding success in the toughest of endurance competitions such as the Paris–Dakar. This, the KTM X-Bow, is the company's first-ever shot at making a car. From these pictures, it looks like they've got a flair for four wheels too. The X-Bow was originally developed in collaboration with Audi, but KTM's insistence on keeping the X-Bow pure and raw meant that Audi chose to limit its involvement to the powertrain. This still means that the X-Bow is powered by Audi's TFSI engine that in basic spec develops 220bhp. Race-inspired design and lightweight materials keep the X-Bow's weight down to around 700kg which promises 0–60mph in a shade under four seconds. The one thing KTM does know a thing or two about is creating an experience. That's why there are no doors, roof, or windscreen on the X-Bow, and little in the way of electronic assistance and comfort. Phenomenal performance on the track, hardcore looks for the street.

Statistics

Type of vehicle:	no frills sportscar
Year:	2006
Country of origin:	Austria
Length:	3670mm
Width:	1870mm
Height:	1160mm
Weight:	721kg
Engine type:	2.0-litre four-cylinder
Max power:	220bhp
Max speed:	135mph
Number of seats:	2
Special features:	hard core looks
Extreme rating:	8

Lexus
Minority Report

Lexus
Minority Report

Wouldn't it be great to take a look at this stunning Lexus again in the year 2054 and compare it to what people are actually driving around in? It's tricky predicting what'll be happening in 10 years' time, never mind 50, but if the Lexus that appeared in the futuristic blockbuster *Minority Report* is anything to go by, then cars will still look pretty cool. Film director Steven Spielberg invited Lexus to come up with a vision of the future – clearly impressed by the Lexus SUV he had in his own garage. Working alongside renowned conceptual artist Harald Belker, the production team devised two transport systems. In built-up areas, a system of pods would scale buildings and other vertical surfaces using magnetic and electrical fields, while this two-seat sportscar was devised for those scenes calling for Tom Cruise's character to drive outside the city limits. It might have been the less extreme of the two, but the cab-forward seating and aggressive lines were a perfect match for this action sci-fi thriller. And with other features such as heads-up instrumentation, night vision, organic recognition, colour-selectable body panels, and auto valet, the car became an overnight movie star.

Statistics

Type of vehicle:	futuristic sports coupé
Year:	2054 (OK 2002)
Country of origin:	USA
Length:	3700mm
Width:	2082mm
Height:	-
Weight:	1043kg
Engine type:	smart recharging electric engine
Max power:	500kW
Max speed:	125mph
Number of seats:	2
Special features:	solar panels for recharging, night vision, laser-guided cruise control, DNA recognition capability
Extreme rating:	5

Maybach
Exelero

Maybach
Exelero

If Darth Vader drove a car, it would be the Maybach Exelero. Nothing else in the galaxy can match the imperious styling, crushing dimensions, and time-warping speed of this one-off custom-built performance coupé. The purpose of the Exelero was to serve as a high-speed test vehicle to showcase a new ultra-high-performance tyre from leading tyre manufacturer Fulda. The car's shape was the brainchild of 24-year-old transport design student Fredrik Burchhardt and the car was built by Stola in Turin. The Exelero retains the supple lines of classic 1930s streamliners, but you need to remind yourself that it has an unladen weight of 2.66 tons and stretches almost six metres in length. To get this gargantuan to the target 350km/h (218mph) was going to require something a bit special. The standard 550bhp V12 engine used in the Maybach saloons was bored out to 5.9 litres, and tuned for 700bhp and over 738lb ft of torque. Kitted out with a full-spec interior, including leather, neoprene, aluminium and carbon-fibre finishes, the Exelero arrived for test at the Nardo high-speed oval where it thundered to a speed of 218.38mph with DTM supremo Klaus Ludwig at the wheel.

Statistics

Type of vehicle:	two-seater coupé
Year:	2005
Country of origin:	Germany
Length:	5834mm
Width:	2120mm
Height:	1376mm
Weight:	2660kg
Engine size:	5908cc
Engine config:	V12 twin turbo
Max power:	700bhp
Max speed:	218mph
Number of seats:	2
Special features:	streamliner styling
Extreme rating:	8

McLean
Monowheel

McLEAN WHEEL

McLean
Monowheel

The world would be a far less colourful
place without the likes of Kerry
McLean. The welder and fabricator
from Walled Lake, Michigan, built
his first monowheel in 1970 and has been
perfecting the design of these elegant and
beautifully engineered vehicles ever since. The
rider and engine sit on an inner metal circle, while the engine drives the
larger diameter circle – which moves independantly of the inner. Steering
is achieved through movement of the the rider's bodyweight. This
particular monowheel is capable of some 35mph, which may not sound
that fast, but represents a major achievement given that monowheels
are notoriously difficult to control. Kerry is also responsible for building
the fastest monowheel ever, clocking 53mph on the Bonneville salt flats
with a 40bhp two-stroke twin. And then there's the McLean V8 – probably
the most extreme monowheel ever created. Amazingly, the V8 powered
monowheel is road legal – which is always good for a few laughs with
Kerry decked out in trademark shades, bandana and leather cut-offs.

Statistics

Type of vehicle:	**monowheel**
Year:	**2000**
Country of origin:	**USA**
Diameter:	**1270mm**
Weight:	**62kg**
Engine type:	**206cc single-cylinder**
Max power:	**10bhp**
Max speed:	**35mph**
Number of seats:	**1**
Extreme rating:	**9**

Mercedes-Benz
F300 Life-Jet

Mercedes-Benz
F300 Life-Jet

The idea behind the F300 Life-Jet, presented at the 1997 Frankfurt Motor Show, was to combine all the best elements of a motorbike with those of a car. Leaning into corners and feeling the power of the engine give the feeling of riding a motorbike, while the Life-Jet's car side brings greater stability thanks to its three wheels, a roof, seatbelts – even air conditioning. It's almost a new species of vehicle. And you don't need a helmet or protective clothing to drive it. Using electronics and hydraulics, Mercedes created a unique Active Tilt Control suspension for the vehicle, so it can lean dramatically into corners with minimum body roll, together with specially developed tyres that give it limpet-like roadholding to match. The suspension also triggers special tilting lights that follow the line of the road as the Life-Jet powers round tricky corners . At the heart of the car, though, is proven hardware in the form of a 1.6-litre A-Class engine positioned at the back. The aluminium chassis weighs in at a mere 89kg, while the aerospace-inspired body offers both upward-pivoting doors and a roof section that can be removed for perhaps the ultimate in open-air car thrills. Just a shame you can't march into your nearest Mercedes showroom and order one quite yet.

Statistics

Type of vehicle:	sports car/motorbike hybrid three-wheeler
Year:	1997
Country of origin:	Germany
Length:	3854mm
Width:	1730mm
Height:	1527mm
Weight:	800kg
Engine type:	1.6-litre four-cylinder, petrol
Max power:	102bhp
Max speed:	132mph (0–62mph in 7.7sec)
Number of seats:	2 (in tandem)
Special features:	computer-controlled headlamp, G-force limiting tilt suspension
Extreme rating:	8

Mini
XXL

Mini
XXL

There's nothing special about a stretch limo these days – they're backed-up behind one another on a Saturday night trading on stag and hen night duty. However, take the trendiest car on the market and give that the Mr Fantastic stretch treatment and we're talking a whole new ball game of fun. Okay, it's not the longest car out there – there's a stretch in LA that's 100-foot long and has, count them, 26 wheels. But the six-wheel, six-seater Mini XXL features the full John Cooper Works tuning kit and was built by a specialist coachbuilder in LA. It comes fully loaded with flat screen TV, DVD and air-con, but the undoubted highlight is the jacuzzi/whirlpool in the rear of the car that comfortably holds two people and features a detachable roof so it can be covered when not in use. THe weight of all that water must play havoc with the steering and handling although an extra axle has been grafted on at the rear. Following its launch in Athens after the Olympic Games, the XXL went on a worldwide tour taking in Australia before flying to Japan and Europe. Stag nights are unlikely.

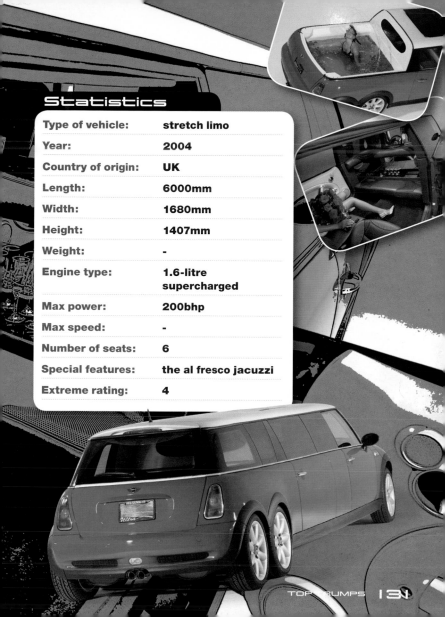

Statistics

Type of vehicle:	stretch limo
Year:	2004
Country of origin:	UK
Length:	6000mm
Width:	1680mm
Height:	1407mm
Weight:	-
Engine type:	1.6-litre supercharged
Max power:	200bhp
Max speed:	-
Number of seats:	6
Special features:	the al fresco jacuzzi
Extreme rating:	4

PAL-V

NEW YORK STATE
DEPARTMENT OF HEALTH

CERTIFIED

PAL-V

The Personal Air and Land Vehicle (PAL-V) is the brainchild of John Bakker who has invested six years of his life developing a concept that can fly as well as drive. Yes, it still looks very much like 'work in progress' but these things take a lot of cash to get off the ground. And who wouldn't want to give one of these a go? According to the Dutch company, the slim, aerodynamic three-wheeler is as comfortable as a luxury car but with the agility of a motorbike thanks to its tilting system. The single rotor and propeller are folded away until the PAL-V is ready to fly – even so the PAL-V will be good for over 125mph and sprint to 62mph in less than five seconds. So far so good. Like a helicopter, PAL-V has a very short take off and vertical landing capability meaning it can land almost anywhere. And because it flies below 4,000 feet, you wouldn't need to file a flight plan. Imagine the chaos. With airspeed to match road speed figures, the potential for PAL-V or its like is huge. What's more, it can run on petrol like a conventional car but also biodiesel or bio-ethanol. All you'd need apart from a driving licence is a sports aviation licence. So hope that the Flying Dutchman gets the backing he deserves.

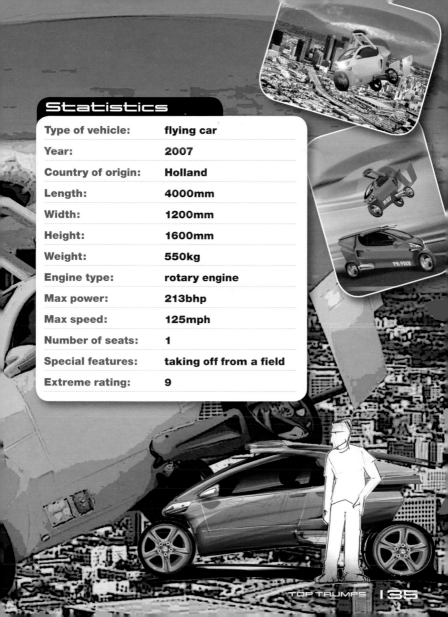

Statistics

Type of vehicle:	flying car
Year:	2007
Country of origin:	Holland
Length:	4000mm
Width:	1200mm
Height:	1600mm
Weight:	550kg
Engine type:	rotary engine
Max power:	213bhp
Max speed:	125mph
Number of seats:	1
Special features:	taking off from a field
Extreme rating:	9

Nissan Pivo

Nissan Pivo

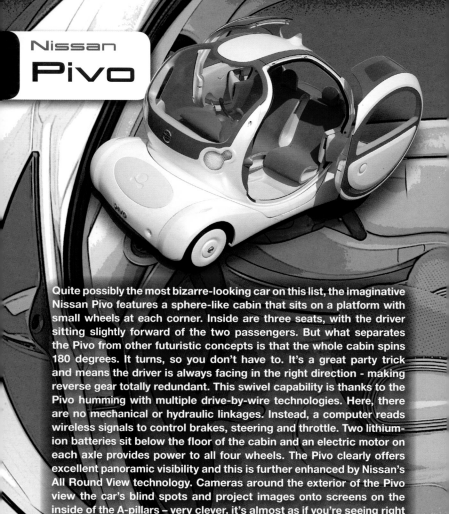

Quite possibly the most bizarre-looking car on this list, the imaginative Nissan Pivo features a sphere-like cabin that sits on a platform with small wheels at each corner. Inside are three seats, with the driver sitting slightly forward of the two passengers. But what separates the Pivo from other futuristic concepts is that the whole cabin spins 180 degrees. It turns, so you don't have to. It's a great party trick and means the driver is always facing in the right direction - making reverse gear totally redundant. This swivel capability is thanks to the Pivo humming with multiple drive-by-wire technologies. Here, there are no mechanical or hydraulic linkages. Instead, a computer reads wireless signals to control brakes, steering and throttle. Two lithium-ion batteries sit below the floor of the cabin and an electric motor on each axle provides power to all four wheels. The Pivo clearly offers excellent panoramic visibility and this is further enhanced by Nissan's All Round View technology. Cameras around the exterior of the Pivo view the car's blind spots and project images onto screens on the inside of the A-pillars – very clever, it's almost as if you're seeing right through the pillar. Definitely an oddball but then it was designed in partnership with Japanese artist Takashi Murakami.

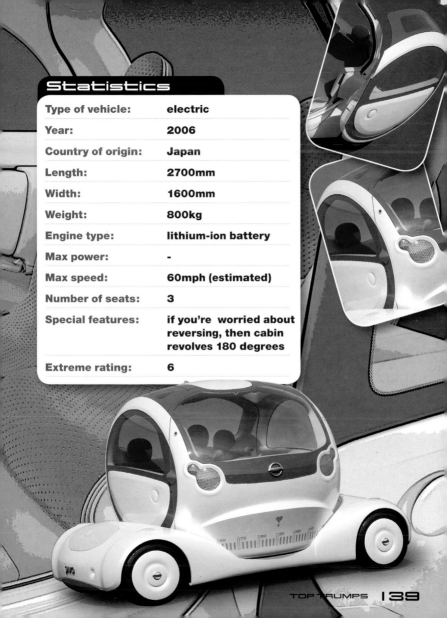

Statistics

Type of vehicle:	electric
Year:	2006
Country of origin:	Japan
Length:	2700mm
Width:	1600mm
Weight:	800kg
Engine type:	lithium-ion battery
Max power:	-
Max speed:	60mph (estimated)
Number of seats:	3
Special features:	if you're worried about reversing, then cabin revolves 180 degrees
Extreme rating:	6

Renault
Espace F1

Renault
Espace F1

How much fun would a family day out be in this? Okay, you'd have to sacrifice a bit on luggage space. And you'd also need to wear full racing gear and helmet. And mum and dad's insurance premium might be a bit steep. But for the chance to ride in an MPV that can destroy 0–60 in 2.8sec and reach nearly 200mph, I'm guessing you'd be prepared to make exceptions. The Renault Espace F1 was first shown at the Paris Motor Show in 1994. This strange alliance of grand prix racing and spacious family motoring came about thanks to Renault's stunning success with Williams in the Formula 1 world championship, and the fact that 1994 marked the 10th anniversary of the launch of the revolutionary Espace. Even so, it still took some imagination to decide on dropping a 3.5-litre V10 F1 engine into the shell of an Espace fresh off the assembly line. The floor was replaced with a carbon body structure housing the 820bhp engine, sequential gearbox and automatic attitude control, while a special front end, massive brakes and aerodynamic wings stopped it taking off. Even today, it's an awesome thing but to fully appreciate the Espace F1, you need to see and hear it. Check out youtube.com for a track day with no less than Alain Prost at the wheel.

Statistics

Type of vehicle:	minivan
Year:	1994
Country of origin:	France
Length:	4430mm
Width:	2057mm
Weight:	1300kg
Engine size:	3.5 litre
Engine type:	V10 Renault Williams RS4 F1 engine
Max power:	800bhp
Max speed:	194mph
Number of seats:	2
Special features:	accelerate from 0–170mph and back to 0 in 600 metres!
Extreme rating:	9

Renault Zoom

Renault Zoom

Pity those poor models all togged out in their futuristic shiny clothes and wraparound sunglasses. It's 1992 and Renault are showcasing the Renault Zoom – an urban concept car that utilises electric power. That power source alone made this quite a forward-thinking venture. But get this: how often do you get a car that boasts two different lengths in the specification list? Okay, Toyota's PM concept lengthens as speed increases, but that was unveiled in 2003 – 11 years after the Zoom. At rest, the Zoom settled into a parking space friendly 2.3m. As its width remains the same, the height clearly has to give and the Zoom grew 23cm taller in this configuration. With a powerplant that offered a nominal 33bhp, the Zoom was certainly confined to the urban environment. However, it certainly had its eye on the future with its hands-free phone and navigation system. Perhaps best of all were the beetle-wing doors. They'd be perfect for those tight parking situations – particularly if your movement is restricted by a shiny suit.

Type of vehicle:	city car
Year:	1992
Country of origin:	France
Length:	2300–2650mm
Width:	1520mm
Weight:	-
Engine type:	electric
Max power:	33bhp (25kW)
Max speed:	-
Number of seats:	2
Special features:	body length and height change depending on driving conditions
Extreme rating:	4

Rinspeed
eXasis

Rinspeed
eXasis

You can always rely on the imagination of Rinspeed founder Frank Rinderknecht to come up with something that breaks the mould and explores new ideas about the way we get around. And the Swiss-based design house didn't let anyone down at the 2007 Geneva Show with the debut of the Rinspeed eXasis – a drivable tandem two-seater with a see-through body and floor. The car marked the 30th anniversary of Rinspeed, and is the result of a collaboration with plastics experts at Bayer MaterialScience AG who produced the transparent polycarbonate. And it looks amazing. The insect-like design with exposed wheels is powered by a highly visible turbocharged 750cc twin-cylinder engine that produces 150bhp and runs on bioethanol. That may not sound much, but the aluminium chassis and lightweight construction weigh in at just 750kg, that's power enough for the eXasis to scuttle from 0 to 60mph in under five seconds. The occupants sit in transparent tandem seats designed by Recaro, while even the instrument panels are transparent and seemingly hover either side of the steering wheel. And of course, glancing down through the transparent floor as the car is moving should provide a special kind of experience.

Type of vehicle:	transparent tandem
Year:	2007
Country of origin:	Switzerland
Length:	3700mm
Width:	1960mm
Height:	1284mm
Weight:	750kg
Engine type:	turbocharged 750cc twin cylinder
Max power:	150bhp
Max speed:	131mph
Number of seats:	2
Special features:	isn't it clear?
Extreme rating:	8

Rinspeed Splash

Rinspeed
Splash

In truth, we could have filled a fair few pages of this book with the automotive creations that have roared out of the fertile imagination of Frank Rinderknecht, boss of Rinspeed. All of his vehicles are off the scale, but any vehicle that can transform from a sportscar to amphibious vehicle at the touch of a button deserves a special mention. The brains behind the Rinspeed Splash is an electronically controlled hydraulic system which deploys a system of hydrofoils that are part of the body of the Splash. The rear spoiler rotates down to rest below the Splash, while hydrofoils either side of the car's body pop out and unfold into a lifting V-shape. With the propeller in place, the Splash is ready to operate as a true hydrofoil about 60cm above the water. On smooth water the Splash is capable of 45 knots (50mph) while it can also operate with retracted hydrofoils as a conventional amphibious vehicle. Even then, it's still quick enough to keep a water skier happy. The Splash is powered by an environmentally friendly turbocharged natural-gas engine that delivers a maximum power output of 140bhp. It's no slouch on the road either. The quick-change artist accelerates in about 5.9 seconds to 62mph and reaches a top speed of 125mph.

Type of vehicle:	**amphibious**
Year:	**2004**
Country of origin:	**Switzerland**
Length:	**3760mm**
Width:	**1865mm**
Height:	**1230mm**
Weight:	**825kg**
Engine type:	**turbocharged 750cc natural gas**
Max power:	**140bhp**
Max speed:	**125mph on land 45 knots (50mph) on water**
Number of seats:	**2**
Special features:	**genius hydrofoil system**
Extreme rating:	**9**

Tango
T600

Tango
T600

Just in case you don't get it from the photographs, the Tango T600 is less than one metre wide – so narrow that you could fit four in a normal size parking space, or drive two side-by-side on a regular one-lane road. But don't be fooled by its rather precarious looks. Rather than being prone to tipping over, this two-seater electric car is as stable as the lowest slung sports car thanks to a hefty battery in the floor of the car. What's even more incredible is that it performs and handles like a sportscar too. The carbon fibre-bodied Tango will accelerate from 0 to 60mph in a mind-blowing four seconds and go on to 130mph – all in the one gear. The Tango has an 80-mile range an can be fully charged in less than three hours. It was enough to convince George Clooney to buy one. The T600 costs $108,000 although a $40,000 model is in development. In many ways, the Tango has the solution for congestion, parking and pollution. All it needs is for the world to catch up to the idea that size is everything.

Statistics

Type of vehicle:	electric
Year:	2006
Country of origin:	USA
Length:	2570mm
Width:	990mm
Height:	1520mm
Weight:	1364kg
Engine type:	electric
Max power:	-
Max speed:	130mph
Number of seats:	2
Special features:	George Clooney owns one
Extreme rating:	8

Tesla
Roadster

Tesla
Roadster

For too long, driving a car with an environmental conscience has been about as exciting as drinking probiotic yoghurt. Thankfully, there's a new batch of cars in production that will radically change that view. And top of that list is the all-electric Tesla Roadster. It's already won heaps of awards for innovation and is one of the most thrilling ways to burn rubber without burning petrol. The revolutionary lithium ion battery pack catapults the Roadster from 0 to 60mph in around four seconds – faster than all but a few supercars – with a top speed of 135mph and a range of 200 miles. And all for an estimated two cents per mile. The first cars to reach the road will be priced at around $92,000, although the plan is to apply the technology to more affordable saloons and mass market models. Although Tesla's HQ is in sunny California, the Roadster is assembled by Lotus Cars in the UK. Indeed, Lotus developed the Roadster style which gives it the classic looks of a sportscar. There's also no need to worry about battery life. It's good for 100,000 miles, after which it can be recycled. Naturally.

Statistics

Type of vehicle:	two-seat, open-top electric sportscar
Year:	2006
Country of origin:	USA
Length:	3946mm
Width:	1873mm
Height:	1127mm
Weight:	1220kg
Engine type:	electric
Max power:	248bhp (185kW)
Max speed:	135mph
Number of seats:	2
Special features:	visual appeal
Extreme rating:	8

Toyota
i-Unit

Toyota
i-Unit

So you're driving along in your i-Unit at a steady 30mph when you see a couple of mates. A touch of a button transforms your low-slung, reclined 'high-speed' mode i-Unit into an upright mode. Now you're able to have a face-to-face conversation with said friends. And that's what this wearable vehicle is all about – transport that enables you to interact with other people. And with a body that's built using environmentally friendly plant-based materials, it's heart is in the right place too. This concept uses drive-by-wire technology and is controlled by joystick-style devices in the armrests. In the upright position, the i-Unit can turn on its spot, while in high-speed mode electric motors in the rear wheels will power the 180kg i-Unit to a giddy 30mph. The driver support system features Intelligent Transport System (ITS) technology, which Toyota hopes to utilize for an accident-free society. The system permits efficient and safe autopilot driving in specially equipped lanes. The one-seat design focuses on interactive communication and is geared towards maintaining contact with the outside world. Each i-Unit has a profile and can be customised to your preferences.

Statistics

Type of vehicle:	personal mobility concept
Year:	2005
Country of origin:	Japan
Length:	1100–1800mm
Width:	1040mm
Height:	1250–1800mm
Weight:	180kg
Engine type:	lithium ion battery, in-wheel motors
Max power:	-
Max speed:	30mph
Number of seats:	1
Special features:	turns on the spot
Extreme rating:	6

Toyota
Volta

Toyota Volta

The Toyota Volta would make the shortlist if for no other reason than it managed to use the words 'eco' and 'supercar' in the same breath. The eco part of the equation for this 2004 concept comes from Toyota's latest Hybrid Synergy Drive, a 3.3-litre V6 petrol engine and two powerful electric motors – one for each axle. The supercar part you can see for yourself, and was penned by Italdesign's Fabrizio Giugiaro – son of design legend Giorgetto. Lightweight? You betcha. The chassis is made from carbon fibre which, coupled with 408bhp of drive, produces a staggering 0–60mph in 4.03 secs and a top speed limited to 155mph. Of course, it wouldn't really be a Toyota unless it was economical too. So fill up the 13.7 gallon tank and you'll be good for 435 miles at motorway speeds. And you can bring two friends in this supercar. With no driveshaft required to the front axle, the flat floor provides room for three seats. And it gets even better. By using fly-by-wire technology, the pedal board and steering wheel can slide to the left and right so everyone gets a go at driving.

Statistics

Type of vehicle:	eco supercar
Year:	2004
Country of origin:	Japan
Length:	4358mm
Width:	1925mm
Height:	1140mm
Weight:	1250kg
Engine type:	3.3-litre V6 hybrid
Max power:	408bhp (300kW)
Max speed:	155mph (limited)
Number of seats:	3
Special features:	flat floor provides seating for three
Extreme rating:	6

GE·203 04

Tramontana

Tramontana

Go on, how big do you reckon this car is? Pictures can be deceiving but it's only a 1+1 seat configuration after all, and there's no boot. Well, the Tramontana occupies the same road space as a Mercedes S-Class – thanks, in part, to those huge side pods that cool the rear-mounted V12 engine. That said, the Tramontana is an extraordinary car. Perhaps the most unusual thing is that it's been developed by a small company based in Girona on the Costa Brava – a region not known as a hotbed of sports car design. But those designers and engineers have pursued their own ideas and created a truly distinctive car that combines the aesthetics of a fighter plane with those of an open-wheel race car. It's one of those cars that just looks fast. And it is. Powered by a twin-turbo V12, the car develops 545bhp or 712bhp (selectable through a switch on the dash) and is built around an F1-style carbon-fibre monocoque construction with ultra-lightweight magnesium components. Buyers of this beautifully crafted car – of which there will only be 12 a year – can then choose to customise it further with wood, white gold or leather trim. Rest assured, there'll be no more individual a car on the road.

Statistics

Type of vehicle:	fighter plane car
Year:	2007
Country of origin:	Spain
Length:	4900mm
Width:	2080mm
Height:	1300mm
Weight:	1260kg
Engine type:	5.5-litre V12 biturbo
Max power:	712bhp
Max speed:	215mph
0-60:	3.7sec
Number of seats:	2 (1+1)
Special features:	originality
Extreme rating:	8

Venturi
Eclectic

Venturi
Eclectic

French manufacturer Venturi has transformed itself from a low-volume sports car maker into a 21st century carbon neutral company producing some of the most innovative concepts ever to grace a motor show. But while the Venturi Fetish retains the looks of a traditional sportscar, the Eclectic looks like nothing else on the planet. However, being the first car to be powered by renewable energy, the Eclectic is doing more than most to save it. Designed for daily driving in urban areas, the Eclectic is powered by electricity from three sources. The roof is equipped with solar cells to harness the power from the sun, while an integrated wind turbine will capture the power of the wind while the car is at a standstill. Both are supported with a plug-in system. Topped up, the Eclectic has a range of 30 miles with a maximum speed of a steady 30mph. But just think of all that free energy being soaked up when its not in use. Okay, so it looks a little ridiculous (and why no doors?), but the Eclectic is certainly extreme in its environmental stance and has recently moved beyond concept and into limited production.

Statistics

Type of vehicle:	**zero emission electro-solar car**
Year:	**2006**
Country of origin:	**France**
Length:	**2860mm**
Width:	**1850mm**
Height:	**1750**
Weight:	**350kg**
Engine type:	**electric**
Max power:	**-**
Max speed:	**30mph**
Number of seats:	**3**
Special features:	**wind turbine**
Extreme rating:	**4**

VW
Concept T

VW
Concept T

Half sports car, half off-roader – here's an incredible 4x4 coupé concept car from Volkswagen. There aren't any current production sports cars capable of driving off-road but VW claims it's plugged this gap with the Concept T. It rides high above the desert sands it seems able to storm, with enormous dished wheels putting its 241bhp to the shifting terrain. Lift the van-like rear cover off and there's a fifth spare, almost filling what would normally be a boot. The stunning scissor-style doors are mounted on the chunky windscreen frame and, when open, they swing slightly outwards and steeply upwards – making the Concept T look like a ladybird in flight. The exterior mirrors are positioned near the top of the windscreen – they need to be, to give a decent view over the car's bulging rear wheelarches. Dual exhaust outlets are also well away from the ground to avoid getting clogged with flying mud. Outlandish as the car may seem, it includes some well-proven VW technology: power from the front-mounted engine is fed to the wheels by the Volkswagen 4Motion permanent all-wheel drive system – just as it does in many an everyday VW Golf. And just so your granny can feel absolutely at home behind the wheel, there's an automatic mode to the otherwise manual six-speed gearbox.

Statistics

Type of vehicle:	crossover
Year:	2004
Country of origin:	Germany
Length:	4079mm
Width:	1963mm
Height:	1450mm
Weight:	-
Engine type:	3-litre V6, petrol
Max power:	241bhp
Max speed:	144mph (0-60mph in 6.9sec)
Number of seats:	2 or 2+2
Special features:	T-bar roof, 'ladybird' doors
Extreme rating:	7

VW
GolF W12-650

VW
GolF W12-650

The word extreme hardly begins to describe what Volkswagen have recently done to their trusty Golf. Created, presumably, to shock the annual gathering of VW enthusiasts at Worthersee in Austria – the largest GTi festival in Europe by the way – the GTi W12-650 is the most powerful Golf ever. Nothing comes close, or is likely to without the use of dragster technology. As ever, the clue's in the name. The one-off concept uses a mid-mounted bi-turbo W12 engine which produces a whopping 650bhp through the rear wheels. Engineers had to create a unique aluminium frame for the engine to sit on, while the restyled carbon-fibre bodyshell features vents ahead of the rear wheels to keep the engine cool. The roof also houses a cooling scoop to channel air into the radiators. The ride height is 70mm lower than a standard Golf, while the use of underfloor aerodynamic aids including a diffuser keep the car pinned to the road. But although the W12-650 is a little wider, lower and restyled for cooling, it's undeniably related to the long line of Golfs. Okay, now for the performance: the sprint from 0 to 62mph takes a tarmac-shredding 3.7sec while the estimated top speed is nearly 202mph. Go get one.

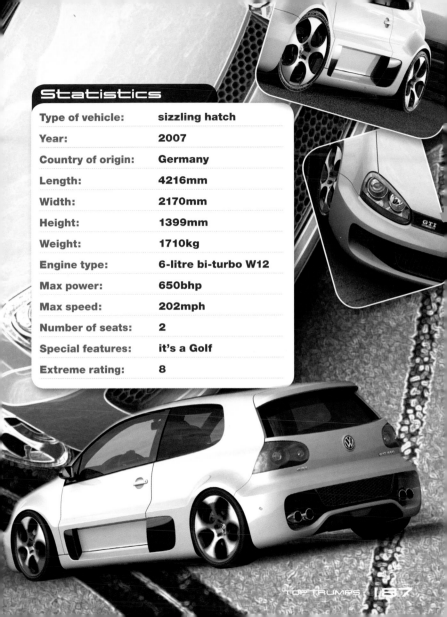

Statistics

Type of vehicle:	sizzling hatch
Year:	2007
Country of origin:	Germany
Length:	4216mm
Width:	2170mm
Height:	1399mm
Weight:	1710kg
Engine type:	6-litre bi-turbo W12
Max power:	650bhp
Max speed:	202mph
Number of seats:	2
Special features:	it's a Golf
Extreme rating:	8